Curriculum Visions **Exp**

Exploring
Britain
vol 1: 1948-1969

1950s school children

1960s school children

The Eagle boys comic goes on sale.
First credit cards in USA.

Teddy boys fashion begins.
Polio vaccination invented.

Roger Bannister breaks
the 4-minute mile.

| **1950** | **1951** | **1952** | **1953** | **1954** |

The Festival of Britain in London.
'The Archers' begins on the radio.

Queen Elizabeth II crowned in June 1953.
Ian Fleming writes about James Bond.

1950s timeline

The kitchen
inside a post-war
'prefab' house.

1960s timeline

World population 3 billion.
1 in 3 British families owns a car.

First James Bond film, 'Dr No', stars Sean Connery.
The Beatles record in Abbey Road studios.

'Top Of The Pops' TV pop music
show begins (and runs to 2006).
First Notting Hill Carnival held.

| **1960** | **1961** | **1962** | **1963** | **1964** |

Soviets Launch First Man in Space
– Yuri Gagarin.
The Beatles appear at the Cavern.

'Dr Who' TV series starts.

The felt-tip pen is introduced.
Bill Haley releases 'Rock Around the Clock'.

Sputnik 1 the first satellite to orbit the Earth is launched by the Russians.

Barbie dolls invented.
The microchip is invented.
First West Indian-style carnival.

1955　　**1956**　　**1957**　　**1958**　　**1959**

First supermarket opens, copying USA style of shopping.

The first stereo LP records are made.
Blue Peter begins on BBC Children's Television.

Contents

Look up the **bold** words in the glossary on page 32 of this book.

The Who's first single is released.
'I Can't Get No Satisfaction…' was the first number one for The Rolling Stones.

The Beatles release 'Sergeant Pepper's Lonely Hearts Club Band' album.

Monty Python's Flying Circus begins.
Americans land on the Moon.

1965　　**1966**　　**1967**　　**1968**　　**1969**

The miniskirt arrives. Star Trek series.
Action Man is invented.
England win the World Cup.

First black woman police officer.
The band Led Zeppelin became famous.

After the war

Our story starts at a time when Britain and her **allies** had just won a world war. But this had left Britain with many problems. Food was short, people were poor and it was a struggle just to survive.

The 1950s and 60s tell us the story of how Britain changed from a time when making a living was difficult, to the time of the 'Swinging 60s', when people could get most of the things they wanted.

When the war ended, millions of soldiers, sailors and airmen came back from overseas and began to start families. As a result, the numbers of babies rose quickly. This is why the years 1946 to 1950 are called the '**baby boom**' years.

During the war women had learnt to do many of the jobs in factories that men had done before the war, so after the war women wanted to be able to go on working. Having two people at work made families much wealthier.

Baby-boom children grew up in a world where TV was not common.

Did you know... ?

- That just after the war coal mines and railways, were **nationalised** by the government.
- Many people lived in temporary homes called '**prefabs**' because their houses had been destroyed by bombing during the war.

Q What happened when the war ended?

Rationing in the 1950s

During the war, Britain had to feed its people from what could be grown on its own farms. This led to shortages. The government controlled how much people could buy of many items. This was called **rationing**.

At the end of the war rationing did not stop straight away. This was because Britain had little money to buy food from other countries.

A whole week's food ration would fit onto one small tray. It was made up of:

1oz cheese; 2oz tea (about 20 teabags worth); 2oz jam; 4oz bacon or ham; 8oz sugar; 1 shilling's worth of meat (a few ounces); and 8oz fats (of which only 2oz could be butter).

By 1946 even bread was rationed. Most rationing went on until 1952, and rationing didn't end until 1954.

Stamping a ration book.

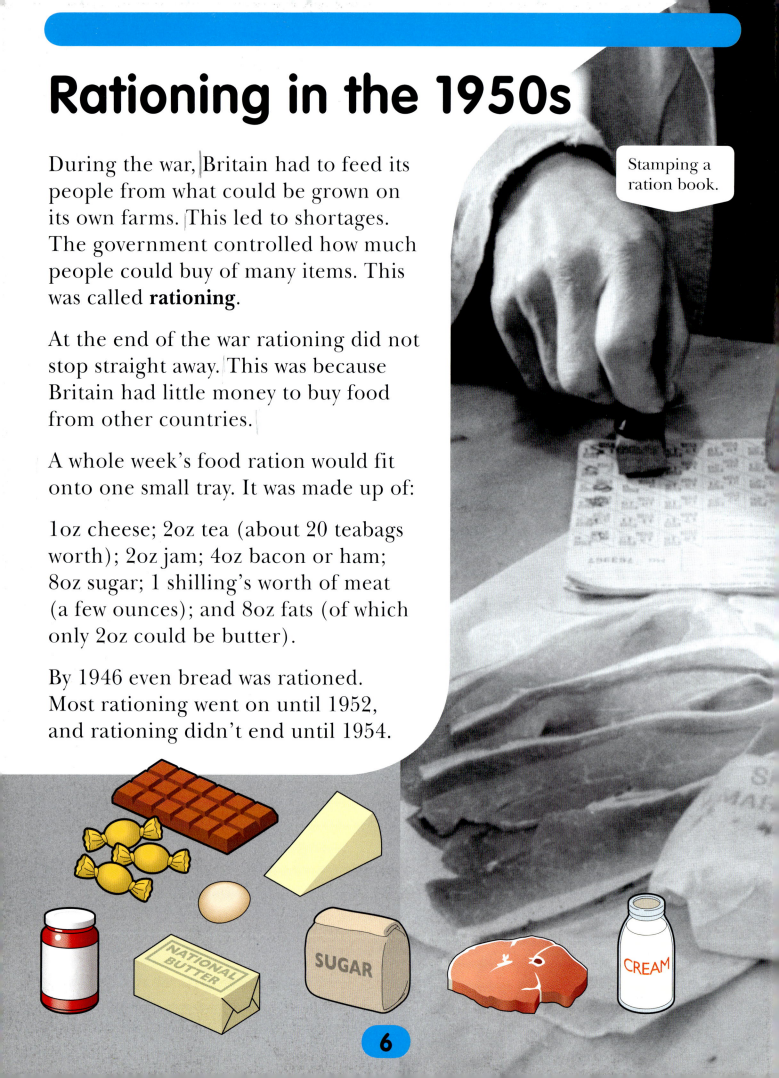

Did you know… ?

- The government planned a new kind of schooling even while the war was on. By the end of the 1940s, secondary schools were divided into three different types: grammar schools; secondary technical schools; and secondary modern schools. This lasted until the comprehensive system started in the 1960s.
- School leaving age became 15 (raised to 16 in 1972).
- Just before the 1950s the government made health care free for all, which is still what happens today. Before that, you had to pay each time you went to see the doctor.

Q Why did rationing go on until the 1950s?

7

New arrivals

Just before the war, Britain had let a large number of people come into the country from Europe. They were running from the Nazis. They included Poles and Jews.

In fact, because Britain had to rebuild its bombed cities, it needed as many workers as it could get, and so extra Europeans were welcome.

But they were not the only ones welcomed to Britain. On 22 June, 1948, nearly 500 people from Jamaica and Trinidad arrived on the SS Empire Windrush. These were the first people from the 'new **colonies'** who, over the next years, were to play such an important part in the life of Britain.

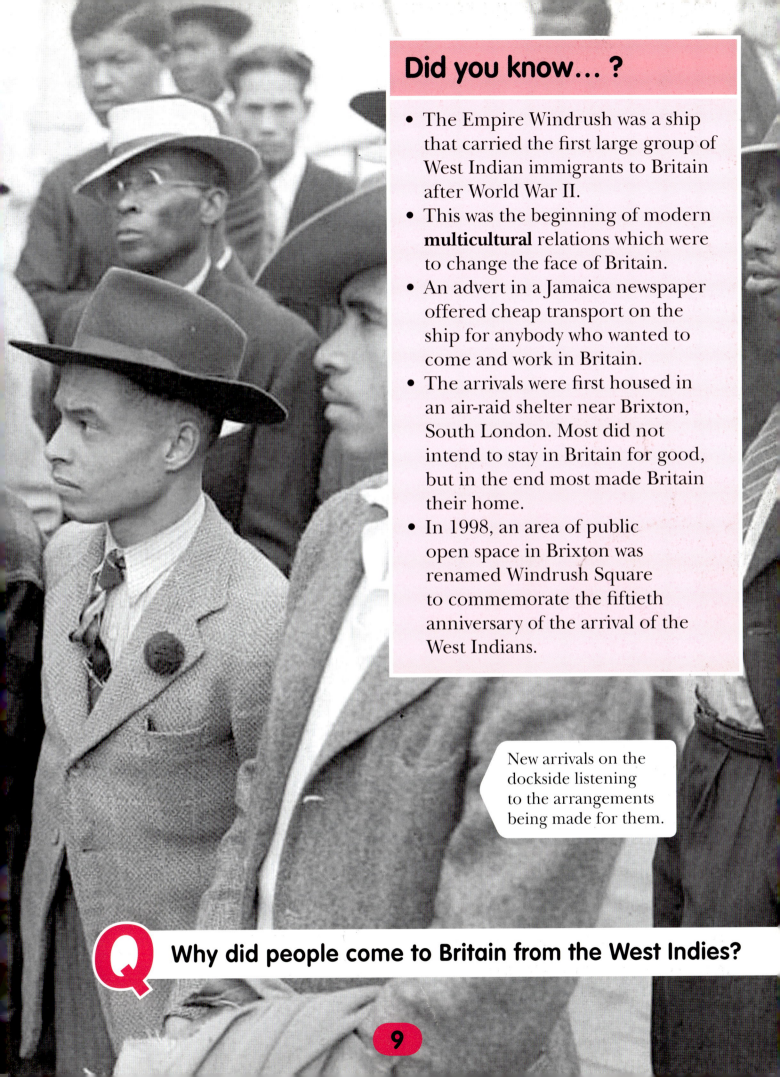

Did you know...?

- The Empire Windrush was a ship that carried the first large group of West Indian immigrants to Britain after World War II.
- This was the beginning of modern **multicultural** relations which were to change the face of Britain.
- An advert in a Jamaica newspaper offered cheap transport on the ship for anybody who wanted to come and work in Britain.
- The arrivals were first housed in an air-raid shelter near Brixton, South London. Most did not intend to stay in Britain for good, but in the end most made Britain their home.
- In 1998, an area of public open space in Brixton was renamed Windrush Square to commemorate the fiftieth anniversary of the arrival of the West Indians.

New arrivals on the dockside listening to the arrangements being made for them.

Q **Why did people come to Britain from the West Indies?**

Britain in the 1950s

When the 1950s started, clothes looked much as they had before the war.

Young people were not interested in fashion. Fashion was only important when people reached their 20s or 30s, or what film stars wore, or people who were very rich.

Most people in the years after the war were not rich, and the money they had only allowed them to buy plain clothes. Children wore school uniforms: a dress for girls, a jacket, cap and short trousers for boys. Girls aged 18 would look just like their mums.

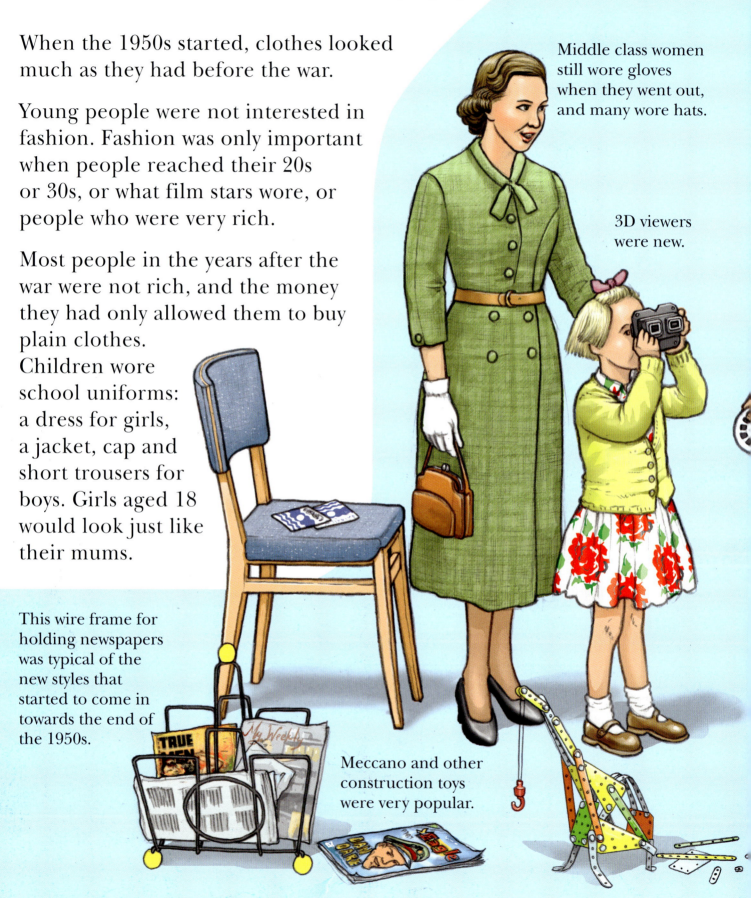

Middle class women still wore gloves when they went out, and many wore hats.

3D viewers were new.

This wire frame for holding newspapers was typical of the new styles that started to come in towards the end of the 1950s.

Meccano and other construction toys were very popular.

10

Middle class men wore suits at home as well as at work.

In the early 50s hair was still a 'short back and sides'. Most boys went to a barber's shop and sat on a plank put on the arms of the barber's chair. Their hair was cut in five minutes.

 Why do you not see any computers in this picture?

Records ran at 78 rpm. A three minute record was as large as a dinner plate. Many gramophones still used metal needles.

It was only late in the 1950s that girls began to dress fashionably, which meant a flared skirt held out by petticoats.

Most men and youths wore jackets and ties – even at home.

Television and wireless

Before the 1950s very few people had televisions. In 1953 Queen Elizabeth II was crowned. Millions crowded around any tiny television set they could find. For many people it was the first time they had seen a television. Just after this, lots of people bought televisions.

Television was very different to today. There was even a gap in programmes during the early evening so that parents could get their children to bed without a fuss!

Q Why do you think people are standing around the TV?

Television, perhaps more than anything else after the war, was to change everyone's lives. It showed things that had never been seen before. For example, it showed places overseas, and it took you into other people's homes. It also showed you what was going on in the news. Before this you only saw 'news' when you went to the cinema. It was shown in the break between films.

Television also showed fashion, so that younger people, in particular, became aware of how others looked.

A 1950s wireless had long, medium and short wave. FM was only just becoming available.

Did you know… ?

- In the 1950s women still wore stockings, and teenagers wore calf-length socks.
- By the mid 1950s women were wearing stiletto heels that were so thin they could make holes in a soft wooden floor!
- The hula hoop was the most widely sold toy of the 1950s with 100 million sold in two years. The frisbee was invented in 1957.
- Because it took so long to make a beehive hair style, some women didn't want to wash their hair regularly. There were even reports of flies nesting in them!

Q Who was the most famous pop star of the 1950s?

The first pop star was middle-aged Bill Haley who sang 'Rock Around the Clock'. But the biggest star of the 1950s was young Elvis Presley. He was the first real rock and roll star. In the 1950s boys wanted to copy Elvis Presley's looks and style, and girls wanted to go out with boys who looked like Elvis.

Teenagers arrive

By the 1950s, people had got bored with drab, plain clothes, but they still didn't have much money.

One cheap and simple way to change their look was to alter hair styles. In the early 1950s pony tails became fashionable. Then hair sprays were invented, which meant that hair could be styled. Even artificial hair pieces could be added to make a design called a beehive.

Then new kinds of clothes arrived for girls. They had tight waists and long skirts that flared out when you twirled around. Later there was the pencil-slim tubular skirt. Then the era of the teddy boys arrived. These were people who dressed in clothes from Edwardian times 50 years earlier. Men wore long 'frock coats' with velvet collars and suede shoes.

Change occurred because young people began to earn good wages, so they had money to spend. As a result, companies took their needs seriously and they were given a new name – teenagers.

1950s shopping

In the 1950s, supermarkets did not exist. If you were to go to a high street grocers, such as Sainsbury's, in the 1950s, you would have gone to quite a small shop with counters down both sides. The counters would have had marble tops and behind them stood assistants waiting to serve you.

You asked for what you wanted, for example, half a pound of butter, and they chopped it off a big block and patted it into shape using wooden paddles, wrapped it and handed it to you. You then paid for it and moved on to the next part of the store where you did this all over again, perhaps buying bacon.

Because all food was fresh and there was no way of keeping it fresh, most people shopped for what they needed each day.

Milk was brought to you each day in bottles by a milkman who might still have a horse-drawn cart.

A typical shop where customers were served by an assistant. At that time assistants could add up the price in their heads of all the goods they sold!

 What were shops like?

Did you know... ?

- In the 1950s families ate more bread, vegetables and milk than most people do today.
- Diets were high in fat. A popular snack was dripping (the fat that comes from cooking meat) spread on bread! Lard (also meat fat) was used for cooking.
- The typical family was still thought of as mum, dad and two children who all ate Sunday lunch. The adverts "Aaah... Bisto", and the Oxo family were some of the first TV advertisements.
- With few fridges and almost no freezers there was no frozen food (such as frozen peas or fish fingers) on sale. People bought what was in season. As a result, you could not, for example, get salad in winter. In winter you bought tinned fruit in syrup.
- Because people did not earn very much, food used up about a third of the weekly wage.

The 1960s begin

In the 1960s many young people changed what they looked like and how they behaved. In the early 1960s some became 'mods' and others became 'rockers' (page 20). Later the style changed to hippy dress. Boys' shirts were brightly coloured and patterned, trousers were tight at the thighs and were flared out so much they hid their shoes (a design based on naval trousers). Jackets and ties were put away – forever.

At the start of the 1960s the only way you could listen to pop records was to listen to Radio Luxembourg (which really did come from Luxembourg because the BBC was the only British broadcaster allowed). Radio Luxembourg had the first DJs and broadcast the first adverts. At the time they refused to play pop records and so pirate radios set up, using ships anchored off the British coast.

In 1967 the government closed them down and re-organised BBC radio into Radios 1, 2, 3 and 4. Radio 1 became the new station for pop music using ex-pirate DJs.

Older people continued to dress in 1950s style.

A new 'modern' style of furniture was made using plastic coverings, but the quality was often poor.

Bell-bottomed trousers and miniskirts became fashionable.

Hair was worn longer than before, and at the end of the 1960s, no boy wanted to be seen in less than shoulder-length hair.

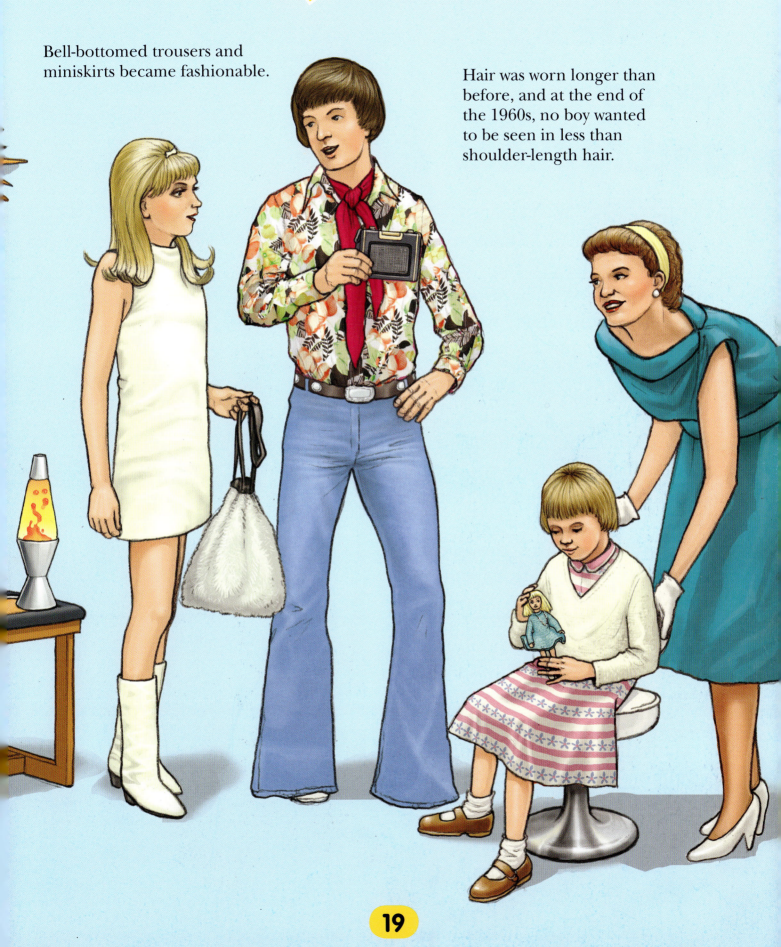

Mods and rockers

From the early 1960s some young people – often those from **working class** backgrounds – began to choose two quite different fashions. They were known as mods and rockers.

The mods rode scooters, mostly lived in city areas, had office jobs and wore what they thought were the latest fashions. They thought the rockers were rough and dirty. The rockers rode motorbikes, stayed with the 1950s styles, mostly had manual jobs and wore leathers. Many of them lived in country areas, and they thought the mods were posh and 'weedy'.

Because these people formed gangs, they sometimes clashed, especially at popular seaside resorts in summer. One famous event in 1964 was even called 'The Second battle of Hastings'.

The 'Battle of Hastings' on the beach in 1964.

Did you know… ?

- Mods wore fashion suits protected by Parka jackets. They rode Vespa or Lambretta scooters fitted out with lots of lights and mirrors.
- The mods and rockers era was over by the mid 1960s. It was replaced by two more clashing groups – the hippies and the skinheads.

Q What was the difference between mods and rockers?

Beatles and boutiques

On 9 February 1961, The Beatles first performed at the Cavern Club in Liverpool. In 1962 they recorded 'Love Me Do' and became an instant success.

The Beatles were the best-selling pop musical group of the 20th century. At the start of the 1960s the most famous pop bands dressed as mods, then, over the years, they gradually changed to hippie styles. The Beatles' 'Sergeant Pepper's Lonely Hearts Club Band' album was the most famous 'hippie' style record of this time.

During the 1960s shops opened which sold only clothes and accessories for young people. These became known as boutiques. As more boutiques were opened, the term 'Swinging 60s' was coined and British fashion led the world.

Boutiques introduced self-service, unlike traditional clothes shops where you had to be served by an assistant. They also played modern music in-store and gave a new and exciting atmosphere to shops.

In Britain the Beatles released more than 40 different singles, albums and **EPs** that reached number one. In 1965 they received the MBE award for services to their country.

Did you know…?

- The 1960s was the time of the miniskirt – which might only be 10 inches (25 cm) long.
- False eyelashes became fashionable and hair was long and straight.
- Plastics were used to make clothes. The 'wet look' PVC was fun to look at, but hot and sweaty to wear. It did not survive into the 1970s.

Q What was different about boutiques?

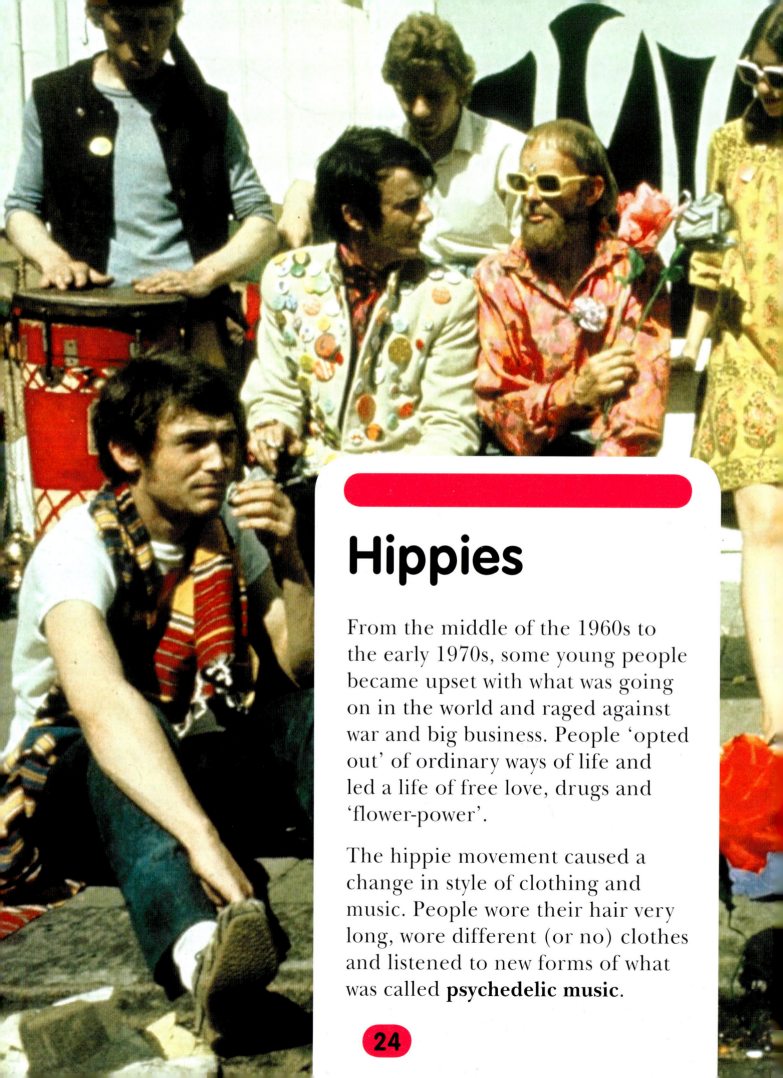

Hippies

From the middle of the 1960s to the early 1970s, some young people became upset with what was going on in the world and raged against war and big business. People 'opted out' of ordinary ways of life and led a life of free love, drugs and 'flower-power'.

The hippie movement caused a change in style of clothing and music. People wore their hair very long, wore different (or no) clothes and listened to new forms of what was called **psychedelic music**.

The CND symbol was a circle with three spokes inside.

Did you know... ?

- During the 1960s there was an **arms race** between the USA and the USSR.
- Some people wanted to try to stop the arms race and destroy all nuclear weapons. One of the main protest movements against the arms race was called CND, the Campaign for Nuclear Disarmament.
- Many people made mass protests and, in the 1960s, an annual march from London to Aldermaston in Berkshire (a centre for nuclear arms research) took place.

1960s TV and radio

In the 1960s it was common for whole families to sit around the TV and watch family programmes. This was the time when new series were launched, some of which still survive. Granada TV launched 'Coronation Street' in 1960. It was the first serial to be shown at dinner time. These programmes were called 'soap operas' because the advertising was often about selling soap flakes to housewives.

ITV (a new channel in the 1960s) competed with the BBC by showing action programmes such as 'Danger Man' and 'Star Trek'.

Television changed the world into a '**global village**' where everyone could see the same thing at the same time. People in Britain saw scenes of war between America and Vietnam, they saw Civil Rights marches in America, and they started to learn about Apartheid in South Africa.

Q Why did people use the term 'soap opera' for programmes like Coronation Street?

A scene from an early episode of Coronation Street.

Did you know… ?

- Television was still new to most people, so many toys were made to copy the stars of the shows. The world's most well-known and best-selling doll was the Barbie doll. Action Man was the favourite boys' toy. He was modelled on a soldier.
- 'Match of the Day' was first broadcast in 1964.
- 1960s young children's television included 'Thunderbirds', 'Andy Pandy', and 'The Flowerpot Men'. For older children there was 'Blue Peter' and 'Dr Who', which began in 1963.

The famous 'cops and robbers' series of the 1960s was Z-cars.

The 'Space Race'

During the 1950s and 60s both the United States and the Soviet Union wanted to be the first into space. The Soviet Union succeeded in 1957 with its tiny satellite called Sputnik 1 and later with cosmonaut Yuri Gagarin. The United States then made an all-out effort to get the first person to the Moon. They succeeded in 1969.

The whole world became excited by this 'Space Race' because they were able to see each step on their new televisions.

Huge amounts of money went into the space race. But this had benefits for everyone because the research produced new kinds of materials, new medicines and new electronic gadgets.

A space song 'Telstar' hit the pop charts and the first words spoken by Neil Armstrong as he stepped onto the Moon, were some of the most famous words ever spoken:

"One small step for man, one giant leap for mankind."

A view of the Apollo 11 lunar module 'Eagle' as it returned from the surface of the Moon to dock with the command module 'Columbia' on 21 July, 1969.

Sputnik, the first object ever to leave the Earth. It was released by the Soviet Union in 1957.

Apollo 11 lunar module pilot, Buzz Aldrin, climbs down the ladder to the Moon's surface as Commander Neil Armstrong photographs his descent. Aldrin became the second person to walk on the Moon.

 Q Who were the first men into space, and who was the first man on the Moon?

The supermarket

Towards the end of the 1950s there had been a shortage of people to work in shops. The government encouraged stores to go self-service, using an idea from America.

Tesco was the first store to try out the idea. Self-service needed a different kind of store, so layouts changed. At the same time stores became much bigger, and later on the word 'superstore' was introduced.

Food was no longer given to you by the assistant, but sold ready-packaged. As a result, makers competed to make their packaging look the most attractive.

Another big change took place in 1964. Before this time, makers set a standard price, and that was what was charged in every store in the country. When this rule was abolished, the big shops like Tesco and Sainsbury's were able to sell more cheaply. The food price war had begun.

Did you know... ?

- In the 1960s, the first cooks were seen on TV (in evening dress!).
- The range of goods in Sainsbury's doubled from 2,000 lines to 4,000 lines during the 1960s.
- People began to take package holidays overseas and so they ate new foods which they wanted to continue eating at home. Spaghetti Bolognese, for example, had never been eaten widely in Britain before the 60s.
- At the same time more Chinese and Asian people arrived, some setting up Chinese and Indian restaurants. They were an immediate success.
- Steamed, sliced white loaf ('Wonderloaf') became popular because it would last longer than oven-baked bread.
- Many people bought refrigerators with small freezing compartments. It was the start of the 'ready meals' era.

A 1960s self-service supermarket. Notice the wire basket – a new feature of such stores. Before that, people had always taken their own shopping bags with them. People had still not got used to a weekly shop and so they bought in relatively small amounts. They also received **Green Shield Stamps**.

Q **What happened when prices were no longer fixed by the makers?**

31

Glossary

allies The people who were on the same side as (allied to) Britain in the Second World War.

arms race A competition between two countries to make sure they have the most up-to-date weapons.

baby boom The period in the late 1940s when there was a large increase in the number of children being born.

colonies Countries that do not govern themselves, but belong to another country.

EP Short for extended play.

global village A term meaning that everyone is now connected so easily using TV, radio and telephone.

Green Shield Stamps These were stamps given when customers bought goods. They could be exchanged for money or presents.

multicultural The idea that a country contains a wide range of people from many countries.

nationalisation To make something the property of a country (nation).

prefab A bungalow meant to be used only for a short while.

psychedelic music Music where the instruments play in a way that tends to flow.

rationing The government instruction to reduce the amount of food everyone could buy. This was necessary during and after the Second World War because food in particular was in short supply and the government wanted to make sure everyone got at least the minimum needed for a healthy diet.

valve A piece of electronic equipment that was used in early radios and TVs.

working class A term that used to be used for people who worked as labourers.

Index

Curriculum Visions

Curriculum Visions Explorers
This series provides straightforward introductions to key worlds and ideas.

You might also be interested in
Our slightly more detailed book, 'Changing Britain vol 1: 1948–1969'. There is a Teacher's Guide to match 'Changing Britain vol 1: 1948–1969'. Additional notes in PDF format are also available from the publisher to support 'Exploring Britain vol 1: 1948–1969'. All of these products are suitable for KS2.

Dedicated Web Site
Watch movies, see many more pictures and read much more in detail about the Second World War and post-war Britain:

www.curriculumvisions.com
(Professional Zone: subscription required)

A CVP Book
Copyright © 2007–2009 Earthscape

First reprint 2009

The right of Brian Knapp to be identified as the author of this work has been asserted by him in accordance with the Copyright, Designs and Patents Act 1988.

Author
Brian Knapp, BSc, PhD

Educational Consultant
JM Smith (former Deputy Head of Wellfield School, Burnley, Lancashire)

Senior Designer
Adele Humphries, BA

Editor
Gillian Gatehouse

Photographs
The Earthscape Picture Library, except *Chiltern Open Air Museum* p2; *Corbis* p14–15, *East Saltoun primary school* p1; *The Imperial War Museum* p4–5 (L044934), 6–7 (D002373); *Mary Evans* p30–31; *NASA* p28–29; *TopFoto* p8–9, 12–13, 16–17, 20–21, 22–23, 24–25.

Illustrations
Mark Stacey, except p6–7 *David Woodroffe*

Designed and produced by
Earthscape

Printed in China by
WKT Company Ltd

Exploring Britain vol 1: 1948–1969
– Curriculum Visions
A CIP record for this book is available from the British Library

ISBN 978 1 86214 217 6